Written by
Lisa DePriest

Illustrated by
Ignacio G.

Copyright © Lisa DePriest 2017
All rights reserved.
Published in the United States by Pet Rescue Books.
No part of this book may be reproduced or transmitted by any means without the written permission of the author.
Printed in China

ISBN: 978-0-9988555-0-9
Library of Congress Control Number: 2017938032
Author photo courtesy of MyPerfectPetPhotography.com
Like us! www.facebook.com/poorteddybook
Visit us! www. PoorTeddyBook.com
Contact us! info@poorteddybook.com

This book is dedicated to:

*My parents, Roland and Flossie Gomez,
for their unconditional love and support.*

*The rest of my family,
Nancy, Lazaro, Daniel, and Amanda Contreras,
Richard Gomez, and Jay Kushner,
for always being there and providing homes to several of my rescues.*

*All of my animal loving friends,
too numerous to mention but likely to appear in future books,
for your friendship and unwavering devotion to the welfare of animals.*

*Last, but not least,
Louis DePriest
for always giving in.*

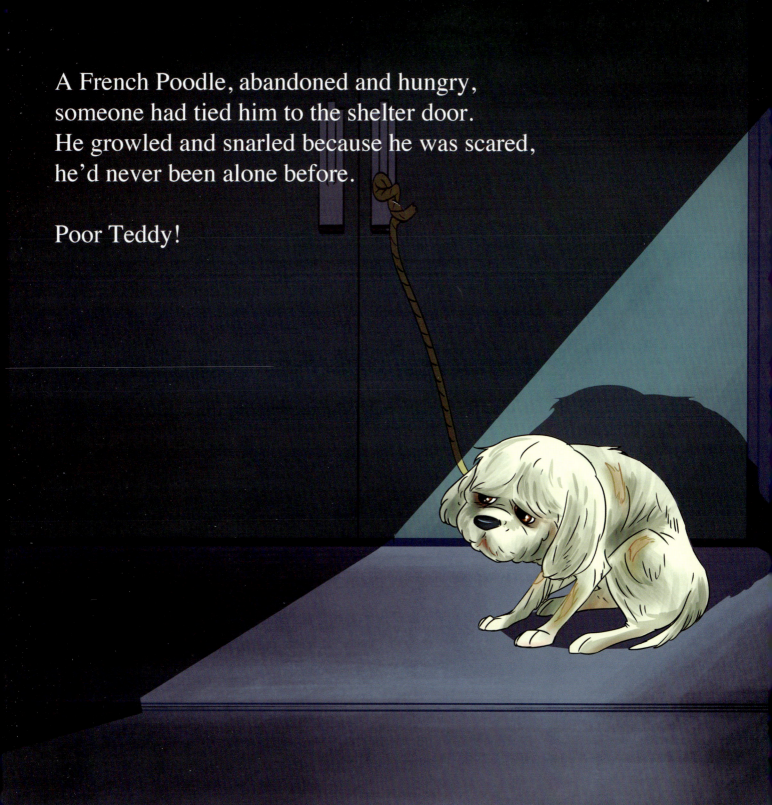

A French Poodle, abandoned and hungry,
someone had tied him to the shelter door.
He growled and snarled because he was scared,
he'd never been alone before.

Poor Teddy!

He squinted his eyes and lowered his head,
as if he were going to be hit.
Even though it seemed like he would,
he never ever bit.

Poor Teddy!

No one knew what his real name was
because he didn't have a tag.
He was abused and so unhappy,
his tail wouldn't even wag.

Poor Teddy!

He was very thin and dirty,
and missing hair in large patches.
Even where he had some hair,
underneath was full of scratches.

Poor Teddy!

The shelter workers cleaned and fed him,
but he was still a little sore.
Once his hair started to grow back a bit,
they put him on the adoption floor.

Weeks later a worker named Lisa
was giving students a shelter tour.
Teddy was frantically running around his pen,
and she was surprised she'd never seen him before.

The students asked, as they passed,
"Why does he keep running? Why is his hair yellow?"
But once they saw other dogs they said,
"Oh, never mind him; look at that cute little fellow."

Poor Teddy!

The running made him dizzy,
so he didn't want to eat.
Because he was running on cement,
he got blisters on his feet.

Poor Teddy!

Lisa felt sorry for him and brought him into her office,
where he finally fell asleep.
He was curled up in a chair next to hers,
And he didn't make a peep.

Lisa's office was down the hall
from Danijela and Kim.
They asked every time they passed her door,
"Any chance you could adopt him?"

Lisa had to leave for the night
and returned Teddy to his run.
He dreamed she'd take him out again tomorrow,
because today was so much fun.

The months passed by
and Teddy remained on the adoption floor.
They took good care of him at the shelter,
but he wanted something more.

"What family would want this little dog?" Lisa wondered,
then thought of Saudi, Titi, and Evie.
She invited them to her house for dinner,
but they canceled; it was raining heavy.

Poor Teddy!

It was too late to return Teddy to the shelter, because it was closed for the night.
He had to spend the night at Lisa's house, and he wasn't about to put up a fight.

So, there Teddy was at Lisa's house, with her two dogs and a cat.
They all got along like family.
Who would have ever believed that?

Lucky was big yet gentle,
even though he was in charge.
Sparky liked to bark a lot,
and wasn't quite as large.

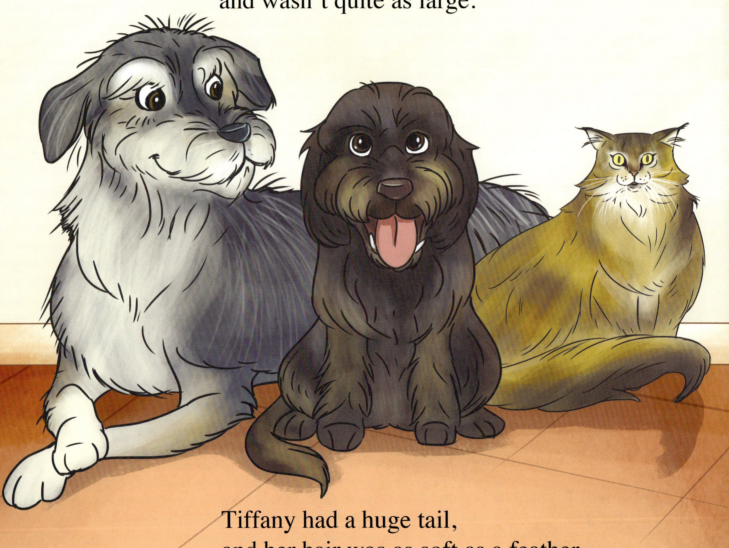

Tiffany had a huge tail,
and her hair was as soft as a feather.
Even though she was a cat,
they got along well together.

Lisa brought Teddy into her room,
and put a bed next to hers on the floor.
Teddy fluffed it up and fell asleep.
He even started to snore!

Whenever Lisa left for work,
all Teddy did was hide.
When she would return home at night,
he wouldn't leave her side.

The house had a big fenced yard,
yet Teddy didn't like to go far.
Except whenever he had the chance,
Teddy loved to take rides in the car.

Although Teddy's skin had improved,
it wasn't all better yet.
Lisa felt she should get another opinion,
so she took him to a new vet.

Teddy met Dr. Paul Cameau,
then Jennifer and Jose.
The doctor recommended some tests,
and Lisa said, "Okay!"

They sent him home with medicine,
and told her, "It might taste funny."
"So, to make sure he will take it,
wrap it in something yummy."

Teddy finished all his medicine,
and was starting to feel great.
Since Lisa still couldn't find a home for him,
all they could do was wait.

Poor Teddy!

Lisa asked the other animals
if they thought Teddy should stay.
They were all rescued too,
So, of course they all said, "Okay!"

They had to ask Louis next,
and they weren't sure what he'd say.
"We have enough pets already!" he exclaimed.
Then he firmly said, "No way!"

Poor Teddy!

After Teddy heard Louis say that,
he knew he had to be smart.
He knew he had to find a way
to win over Louis' heart.

Although at times he seemed grumpy,
Teddy knew that Louis was kind.
Teddy really wanted to stay there
and knew he had to change Louis' mind.

Teddy didn't shed,
and for that, Louis was fond.
But that wasn't quite enough
to make the two of them bond.

Louis threw a ball,
and excitedly said, "Teddy, go get it!"
Teddy didn't understand how to play fetch.
Frustrated, Louis said, "Forget it!"

Poor Teddy!

Teddy knew he had to find something soon on which they could both agree.
He thought and thought and then it hit him; they both liked to watch TV!

Louis would pet Teddy,
while he sat next to him in a chair.
It didn't matter what shows Louis watched,
Teddy didn't care.

Louis liked that it didn't matter,
whether they watched a movie, football, or the news.
If Teddy didn't like what show was on,
he closed his eyes and took a snooze.

Lisa, Lucky, Sparky, and Tiffany asked again if Teddy could stay. Apparently, Teddy finally grew on Louis, because this time he said, "Okay!"

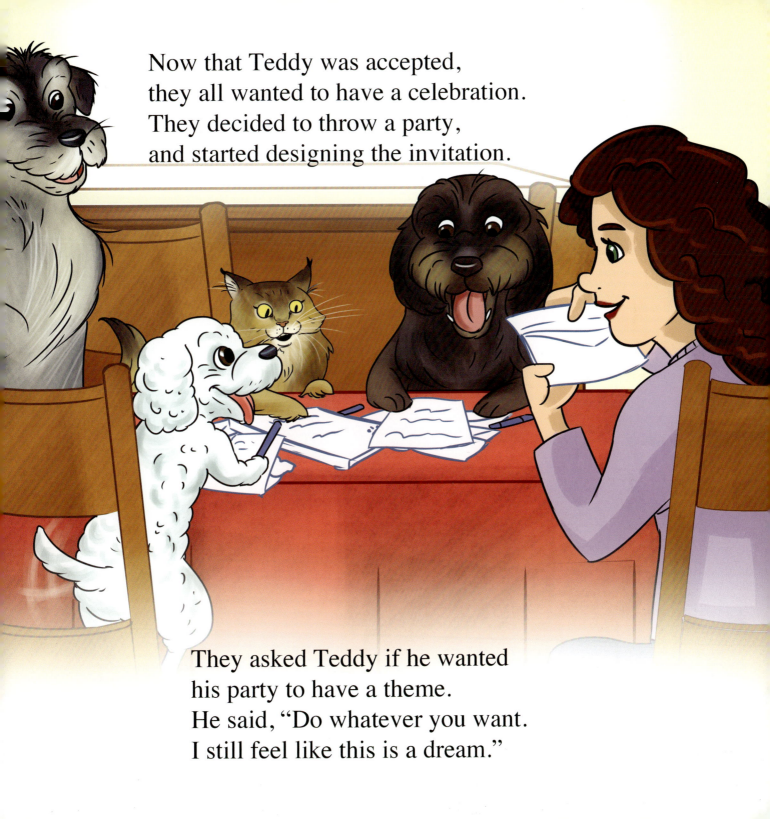

Now that Teddy was accepted,
they all wanted to have a celebration.
They decided to throw a party,
and started designing the invitation.

They asked Teddy if he wanted
his party to have a theme.
He said, "Do whatever you want.
I still feel like this is a dream."

They gave each other silly names,
Lucky the Lookout, Sparky Plugs, and Tiffany the Tail.
As guests began to RSVP, Louis hollered,
"How many did you put in the mail?"

The phone continued to ring and ring,
people saying they would attend.
At one point Louis asked again,
"How many invitations DID you send?"

Teddy was thinking of his shelter friends,
David, Maureen, and Mariagrazia,
when Lisa asked him "What food should we serve?"
"I know!" Teddy exclaimed, "Why not some pasta?"

Teddy wanted to look his best for the party, so he went to get groomed by Elaine. She asked him what style he wanted, and Teddy answered, "Just something plain."

Before Elaine could cut Teddy's hair, he needed a bath from Nucho.
He lathered him up and as he rinsed him off, Teddy whispered, "Te quiero mucho."

Lisa started to prepare the food,
and her mom Flossie gave her a hand.
The party was going to be such fun,
they even hired Manuel's band.

They had a salad bar, a spaghetti bar, and a dessert bar with many sweets. And the guests brought lots of presents, including doggie treats.

As the party went on, Lisa did a head count, and the guests totaled seventy-two.
Lisa kissed the top of Teddy's head and said, "They're all here because of you!"

Poor Teddy?

Toward the end of the night, Lisa gathered the crowd, and that's when the announcement was read.
"This is Teddy's new home!" she said with a smile.
"He even has his own bed!"

Teddy's life turned completely around,
and now nothing was the same.
Therefore, Lisa knew they had to come up
with a much more fitting name.

After much thought, she decided on one,
and asked the crowd, "Are you ready?"
"Because of Teddy's curly hair and our family's
love of pasta, we'll now call him...

Some things may look bad from the outside,
but with patience you can bring out the good.
Love and understanding go a long way,
and before you know it, things will be as they should.

All homeless animals deserve a good home,
that's certainly my wish.
And just because poodles originate from France,
they can still be named after an Italian dish!

There is one more important thing
that I would like you to keep in mind.
Whether it's an animal, person, or Mother Earth,
always remember to be kind!

Lucky 'Lookout'  Sparky 'Plugs'  Tiffany 'the Tail'

invite you to join them in welcoming

Teddy 'Spaghetti' into the Family

What : Spaghetti Bar, Salad Bar and Dessert Bar
Come eat, relax and enjoy the company of good friends and family

Where : 120 Pet Street Miami, FL

When : Saturday February 23   5pm - 7:30 pm

Please RSVP so we order enough food.
555-555-7905   555-555-2111
and whatever you do .... don't

FUGGEDABOUTIT!!!

Lisa DePriest is a lifelong resident of Miami, Florida, and her passion for animals runs in the family. Her first dog, Mopsy, was rescued from the streets when Lisa was only seven years old and he lived for twenty years.
Lisa volunteered at a local animal shelter for many years and received the Dade County Veterinary Foundation Volunteer Award in 2002.
In addition to running her own small business, Basket Hound, she currently works at a local Humane Society educating the public, especially children, on responsible pet ownership. In her spare time Lisa enjoys visiting with friends, watching comedy, and painting, especially pets.
Lisa is a SCBWI member and *Poor Teddy* is her first book to be published. With all of her rescued pets and their stories, it certainly will not be her last.
Lisa currently has four dogs and two cats:
Lucky, Sparky, Teddy, Yogi, Oreo, and Baby - all rescues, of course!